LIFE
LESSONS
for Dad

Tea Parties,
Tutus &
All Things
Pink

MICHAEL MITCHELL

PUBLISHING GROUP
Nashville, Tennessee

Add your own photo
and caption on this page

*Isabella, my little lion,
this book is for you. My
heart started beating
out of my chest the day
you were born, and it's
never going back inside.
You're perfect in every
way. Never forget that.
I love you heaps, Daddy.*

978-1-4336-8277-3

Published by B&H Publishing Group

Nashville, Tennessee

Dewey Decimal Classification: 306.874

Subject Heading: PARENTING \ DAUGHTERS \
FATHER-DAUGHTER RELATIONSHIP

cover photo by Nina Cecilia/Creative Spark

Printed in China

1 2 3 4 5 6 7 8 • 18 17 16 15 14

Remember, no matter what age, she will always be your little girl.

Love her mom. Treat her mother with respect, honor, and a big heaping spoonful of public displays of affection. When she grows up, the odds are good she'll fall in love with and marry someone who treats her much like you treated her mother. Good or bad, that's just the way it is. I'd prefer good.

Always be there. Quality time doesn't happen without quantity time. Hang out together for no other reason than just to be in each other's presence. Be genuinely interested in the things that interest her. She needs her dad to be involved in her life at every stage. Don't just sit idly by while she adds years to her life . . . add life to her years.

Jen Snyder

Though conventional wisdom may suggest otherwise, puddles are to be stomped in, not stepped over. Jumping, dancing, and splashing, while totally optional, are also always appreciated.

Be careful not to dismiss misbehavior when she's a toddler just because it seems cute. What's cute at two is not always so cute at twelve, sixteen, or twenty-one.

Boys will break her heart. So will mean girls, stray puppies, and devastating athletic losses. Be there to help pick up the pieces.

The first time she says the words, "I love you Daddy" will be one of the happiest moments of your life. Don't be surprised if she throws a tantrum a few minutes later. Such is fatherhood.

3 a) $a(7.5) = v'(7.5) = \dfrac{v(8) - v(7)}{8-7} = -.1 \dfrac{miles}{min^2}$

c) $\displaystyle\int_0^{12} \dfrac{\Pi}{5} \sin \dfrac{\Pi}{12} t \, dt$

b) $\displaystyle\int_0^{12} |v(t)| \, dt$ is the total distance traveled in 12 min.

$\displaystyle\int_0^{12} |v(t)| \, dt = \int_0^2 v(t) \, dt - \int_2^4 v(t) \, dt + \int_4^{12} v(t) \, dt$

$= .2 + .2 + 1.4 = 1.8 \, miles$

$\dfrac{\Pi}{5} \displaystyle\int_0^{12} \sin u \, du$

$\cos\left(\dfrac{\Pi}{12} t\right)\Big]_0^{12}$

"If I have seen further than others, it is because I have stood on the shoulders of giants."

She's as smart as any boy. Make sure she knows that.

When she learns to give kisses, she will want to plant them all over your face. Encourage this practice.

Of course you look silly playing peek-a-boo. You should play anyway.

There will come a day when she asks for a puppy. Don't over think it. At least one time in her life, just say, **"Yes."**

It's never too early to start teaching her about money. She will still probably break your bank as a teenager . . . and on her wedding day.

Make pancakes in the shape of her age for breakfast on her birthday. In a pinch, donuts with pink sprinkles and a candle will suffice.

Buy her a pair of Chucks as soon as she starts walking. She won't always want to wear matching shoes with her old man.

Learn to say no. She may not like it today, but someday you'll both be glad you stuck to your guns.

Take her fishing. She will probably squirm more than the worm on your hook. That's okay.

Dance with her. Start when she's a little girl or even when she's a baby. Don't wait until her wedding day.

Annaleise Mitchell

Tell her she's beautiful. Say it over and over again. Someday an animated movie or "beauty" magazine will try to convince her otherwise.

Teach her to change a flat. A tire without air need not be a major panic inducing event in her life. She'll still call you crying the first time it happens.

Do not . . . I repeat . . . do not get rid of a single stuffed animal without asking her permission first. Ignore this warning at your own peril.

Be there to hold her hand as she tries new things throughout her life.

She will fight with her mother. Choose sides wisely.

Go ahead. Buy her those pearls.

Knowing how to eat sunflower seeds correctly will not help her get into a good college. **Teach her anyway.**

She will eagerly await your return home from work in the evenings. Don't be late.

Don't let her see you cry the first time she leaves the house wearing makeup.

Toys, like most things, are only good in moderation. Don't overdo it.

Teach her to roller skate. Watch her confidence soar.

Let her roll around in the grass. It's good for her soul. It's not bad for yours either.

Go along when her mother takes her swimsuit shopping. Don't be afraid to veto some of her choices, but resist the urge to insist on full-body beach pajamas.

She'll probably want to crawl in bed with you after a nightmare. This is a good thing.

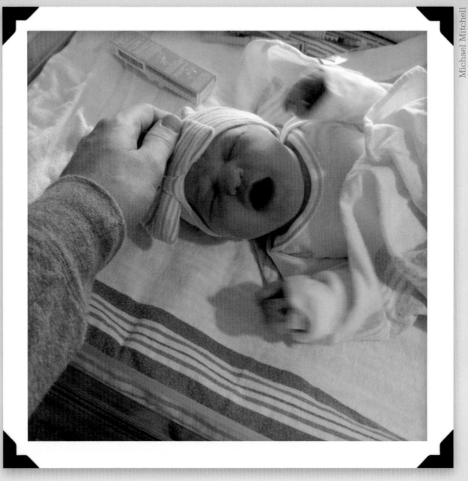

Few things in life are more comforting to a crying little girl than her father's hand. Never forget this.

Shazia Baker

Introduce her to the swings at your local park. She'll squeal for you to push her higher and faster. Her definition of "higher and faster" is probably not the same as yours. Keep that in mind.

Holding her upside down by the legs while she giggles and screams uncontrollably is great for your biceps. WARNING: She has no concept of muscle fatigue.

She might ask you to buy her a pony on her birthday. Unless you live on a farm, **do not** buy her a pony on her birthday. It's okay to rent one.

Stacey Markel

Be very, very careful what you say to your little girl. She will grow up to be exactly who you tell her she is.

She isn't making a mess . . . she's making memories.

Want a confident daughter? Be a nurturing dad. The two are almost always related.

Tell her often that you love her. Those three words will melt her heart.

When she wraps those tiny fingers around one of yours, you will feel like a million bucks. Encourage her to do this often.

Teach her how to swing a hammer. Self-sufficiency is one of the most precious and estimable gifts you can give a little girl.

Teach her to love her siblings, even when they can be a bit bothersome.

Grandparents are very important. Make sure she spends time with them.

Teach her the difference between right and wrong. Do it without yelling.

Take her camping. Immerse her in the great outdoors. Watch her eyes fill with wonder the first time she sees the beauty of wide open spaces. Leave the electronics at home.

Little girls like to wrestle with their dads just as much as little boys. Letting her win does not mean you are less of a man.

Dry her off after bath time. When she lays her clean little head on your shoulder and grabs a piece of your shirt, you will want to freeze time.

It's in her nature to make art and it's quite possible that she may use your living room wall as a canvas. If you always keep an extra can of paint on hand, you'll be much less likely to overreact when this happens.

She may be your little princess, but just remember, even little princesses need a few chores to teach them responsibility.

Tell her how you proposed to her mother.

Don't correct her when she colors outside the lines. This will be a very valuable skill when she's a grown woman.

There is a direct correlation between a girl's self-esteem and the physical affection she receives from her father. In case you're wondering, now would be a good time to drop everything you're doing and go give your daughter a big hug.

The view is always better from atop your shoulders. Remember this at parades, sporting events, and anywhere else she might want to get a better look.

Introduce her to the tickle monster. This will add life to both your years.

Treat her drawings like beautiful works of art. Hang them up in your office. She'll come visit you someday and it may finally hit her just how much you really love everything about her.

If you don't teach her how to do a cannonball into the deep end, who will?

Give her your undivided attention. She can tell if you're distracted.

She will cry. Often. Always have tissues. If a tissue cannot be found, your shoulder is a great substitute.

When work or other obligations force you to leave town without her, make it a priority to Skype together every day. This is as much for your benefit as it is for hers.

What's that you say? You need Daddy to paint your nails? Absolutely!

A living room, a few pieces of furniture, a blanket or two, and a little imagination are all she needs for an afternoon filled with wonder. She already has the imagination. The rest is up to you.

Take her to the big game. Patiently explain the finer points of gridiron strategy. Who says a little girl can't appreciate the game of football?

Take her out for coffee and donuts if she wakes up early on a Saturday morning. Her mother will thank you for the extra time alone.

Brush her hair when she's a little girl. It will be one of her fondest memories someday.

When this happens, do everything in your power to be still and let her sleep. The older she gets, the less opportunities you'll have to be her pillow.

Bridie Murray

Staring contests are a great way to pass the time. Making faces at her will give you the advantage in more ways than one.

Jen Snyder

She will never cease to amaze you with her uncanny ability to make a mess.
Don't overreact.

Teach her to appreciate a good book.

You're never too big to go down the slide with her.

Doing the dishes together is a great way to teach her responsibility. Playing with the bubbles can be bonus points.

Spend lots of time on the floor together. If you're lucky, she will dive bomb you when you least expect it.

Introduce her to the joy of cupcakes. Then again, her mother just might beat you to it.

Teach her to read a map. You won't always be there to show her the way.

Jen Snyder

Introduce her to the joy of the bubble bath beard.

Take her to work with you. Let her see what you do all day while she's off being a kid somewhere. If you're lucky, she'll make it 'til 10 o'clock before telling you she's bored.

Take her on a date. Show her how she should expect to be treated when she turns thirty and can start dating men other than you.

Let her bury you in the sand.

Take her on a hayride during the fall. You might get itchy but you'll build a memory.

A visit to see Mickey is a must, even if her little brother must tag along.

Jamie Freymuth

Encourage her inner rock star. Then again, she may not need any help in this area.

Tuck her into bed, read her a bedtime story, and kiss her goodnight as long as she'll let you.

At least once a month, let her stay up past bedtime so the two of you can spend more time together.

Record your voice singing a lullaby or reading a book for her to listen to while you're away. You can still be part of her bedtime routine even when you can't be there. This will also be something she will cherish when she shares it with her own children.

In those rare moments when one or both of you find yourself at a loss for words, never underestimate the power of simply standing together in silence.

Teach her how to ride a bike. Once the training wheels come off, get out there and explore the world together.

Be her window to the outside world. Bright lights and noise need not be a frightening experience for a young girl.

Jen Snyder

Stand over her crib at night and watch her sleep. This is when life starts to make sense.

Take long walks together. Conversation optional. The older she gets, the more special this experience will be for both of you.

Always give piggyback rides . . . especially before bed. She'll be on your back for other things later.

Take lots of pictures together. You never know when one of you won't be around to smile for the camera anymore.

Jeremy Henry

Be there to pick her up from school as often as possible. Do it now while she's still young enough to greet you like this.

Take her horseback riding and allow her to ride on her own. Cowboy attire is optional.

Take her to the zoo. She'll love the monkeys . . . probably because they remind her of you.

It's okay to indulge her sweet tooth from time to time. Just make sure she eats her vegetables first.

She can run as fast as any boy. She will forget this fact from time to time. It's your job to remind her.

Occasionally surprise her with flowers. The older she gets, the more she'll appreciate this gesture of love.

Someday you will hurt her feelings. The quicker you apologize, the better you'll both feel about it. A verbal, "I'm sorry" is good. A handwritten note is even better.

If you want a strong daughter, teach her to say no and then respect her boundaries.

A chocolate milk shake is a joyful experience at any age. Never forget this.

There's great joy to be found jumping on beds. She'll enjoy it too.

Encourage her to play dress up. It will expand her creativity.

Brad Weaver

Ask about her day when you get home from work. Put down your smart phone and really listen to her answers. This will become one of the best parts of her day.

The safer she feels, the better she'll sleep. Be her safe haven.

Never be afraid to let her explore. This will empower her to conquer the world.

Bake a cake together. Let her lick the spoon when you're done.

The world always needs more female athletes, engineers, scientists, scholars, politicians, entrepreneurs, and humanitarians. Encourage her to pursue her passions.

Jen Snyder

Raking leaves may seem like a chore, but trust me . . . it's not. Just wait 'til you see the look on her face when you dive into the pile first.

Sometimes all she really needs is a little push.

There is great joy to be found in bubble wrap.

Walk her though the many "weeds" that can come in her life. She needs a guiding hand.

Face painting can be fun. Especially when there are unicorns involved.

Imparting critical life skills is one of your most important roles as her dad. Teaching her how to carve a pumpkin is no exception to this rule.

No matter how many times she asks, never lose your patience responding to the question, "Are we there yet?"

Don't be afraid to let her see you cry. She'll appreciate this side of you more than you'll ever know.

As she grows, pray for the man that may propose someday.

Pick out a special daddy daughter ornament together each year. Give them to her someday when she has a Christmas tree of her own.

When the question is, "Hey, Dad?" the answer should always be, "Yes, sweetie?" not, "Hold on a second." You never know how important those seconds might be.

Stacey Markel

Grades are important, but in the end, it's how she treats others that matters most. Remember this the first time she brings home a disappointing report card.

Introduce her to the joy of rolling down hills.

Sing to her. Every day. Even when you don't feel like it. Do it often enough and the sound of your voice will become a permanent source of steadiness in her life.

Learn to trust her. Gradually give her more freedom as she gets older. She will rise to the expectations you set for her.

Take her to feed the animals whenever possible. Especially exotic ones!

Without exception, always answer when she calls. It probably won't be urgent, but when it is, you'll be glad you picked up.

Never drive away without first waving good-bye.

She'll never forget the day you stayed home from work to play in the snow with her. Neither will you.

There will be drama. Oh yes, there will be drama. Don't overreact and everything will eventually work itself out.

Annaleise Mitchell

Being a great dad means knowing the difference between the life lessons you can teach her and those she needs to be allowed to learn on her own.

Be patient with her. In doing so, you will teach her that she's worth waiting for.

The ball pit is a magical, special place. Never underestimate it!

Protect her childhood. It's the only one she's got.

Teach her to jump—fearlessly.

Hold her at night when she's sick and can't sleep.

Teach her to drive a stick shift. She will pop the clutch and grind the gears. Be cool when this happens.

Austin Schroth

Never ask her to do anything you're not willing to do yourself. This rule does not apply to her math homework.

Though she may try to distance herself from you as a teenager, this is when she needs you most. Pursue her.

Ask about her hopes and dreams. Write down her answers so you can help her remember them throughout her life.

Let her hear you bragging about her to others.

Leave little notes in her lunchbox, jacket pockets, or anywhere else you might surprise her during the day.

Make her a homemade card for Valentine's Day. She'll probably make one for you.

Save the day. She'll grow up looking for a hero. It might as well be you. She'll need you to come through for her over and over again throughout her life. Rise to the occasion. **Red cape and blue tights optional.**

Savor every moment you have together. Today she might be crawling around the house in diapers, tomorrow you're handing her the keys to the car, and before you know it, you're walking her down the aisle. Some day soon, hanging out with her old man won't be the bees knees anymore. Life happens pretty fast. You better cherish it while you can.

Remember, if you do have a dog, get one that will allow her to ride or even paint its nails.

You will always be her first Valentine. This role is not to be taken lightly.

For the first few years of her life, her imaginary friends may outnumber her real friends. Do your best to learn their names.

Find a way to captivate her imagination at least once every day.

Write her a short note every day you're away. Making up for lost time is not easy. It's not impossible either.

Ask who her heroes are. You can learn a lot from her answer. Who knows? You may even make the list.

Make a habit of giving her simple, inexpensive gifts. When in doubt, a balloon on a string is always a big hit.

Give her an affectionate nickname that only the two of you know.

While there's no such thing as the perfect dad, if you're present in her life, apologize when you screw up, and shower her with affection, you might get pretty close.

She will skin her knees and stub her toes. Be there with a kiss to make it all better.

Encourage her to make mistakes. No one ever succeeded at anything worthwhile without messing up a few times first.

Despite your best efforts, she may still be a mama's girl for the first few years of her life. Don't lose too much sleep over this. Eventually she'll come around.

Surprise her by saying yes to something you'd normally say no to. Cotton candy before bed, perhaps?

Some morning when it's just the two of you, surprise her with ice cream for breakfast.

Pick a clear night, go outside, and gaze up at the stars together. Show her the Big Dipper, wish upon a star, and let her know that dreams can come true.

Pick one day each year and let her dictate everything you do together.

If you want to be her friend in adulthood, you have to act like her parent today. This rarely works in reverse.

Read to her. Often.

Make it a point to always know who her friends are.

Start saving today for her college tuition.

Try not to be the first one to break a hug.

Let her dress herself from time to time. Who says she always has to match?

When in doubt, ask her mother.

Teach her to climb trees. Don't be surprised if you become increasingly nervous the higher she goes. Encourage her to keep climbing.

Let her get dirty.

Your daughter is a princess. Always be her prince!

Tell her one thing you appreciate about her every day.

A little girl can, at times, seem a lot like a cake that came out of the oven too soon. Beautiful on the outside . . . gooey and messy on the inside. Your job is to help her finish baking.

Girls who are physically active are less likely to engage in promiscuous sexual activity, drop out of school, or put up with abuse. Get her involved in sports at a young age.

Tea parties are a big deal. Do not take them lightly.

Shazia Baker

At times her behavior will seem like a complete and utter mystery. Just remember, much like her mother, your daughter's ways are not your ways.

Sometimes a listening ear is all she needs. For everything else, just smile and fix it.

Slow down. Her little legs can't always cover as much ground as yours.

Luke Noffke

Remember, just like a butterfly, she too will spread her wings and fly some day. Enjoy her caterpillar years.

Jen Snyder

Make sure your face lights up any time she enters the room. Do this throughout her life and she will always feel treasured.

Her charm will always win you over. Remember this when she's misbehaving or asking for something she doesn't need.

Only give her things she asks for politely. Please and thank you should be corner-stones of her vocabulary.

It's okay to buy her dolls. Just make sure you buy plenty of books to go with them.

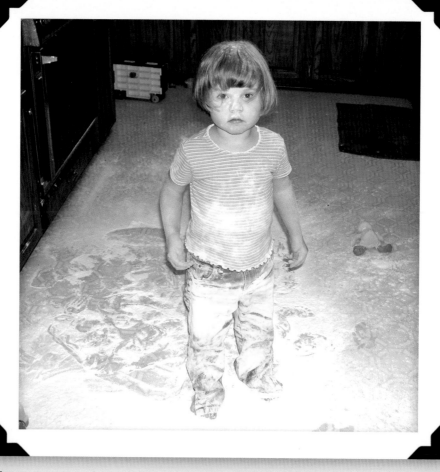

There may come a day when she's especially adept at pressing your buttons. Learn when to press back and when to walk away. If you're unsure, do the latter.

It's okay to make plans for her future. Just remember, it's equally okay for her to ignore them. You wanted a confident daughter, right?

Spend time each day holding her in your arms. A healthy dose of this throughout her childhood will last you both a lifetime.

Make time to play with blocks together. You stack 'em up. She'll knock 'em down.

If her mom enrolls her in swim lessons, make sure you get in the pool too.
Don't be intimidated if there are no other dads there. It's their loss.

Never miss her birthday. In twenty years she won't remember the presents.
She will remember if you weren't there.

Dan King

There's a fine line between being involved in her life and completely smothering her. Even a daddy's girl needs time by herself every now and then.

Tell her you love her not because she's smart or kind or fun or beautiful. Tell her you love her because she's your daughter and there's no one else like her in the entire world.

Let her flex her independence muscle from time to time as a child. The more freedom you give her now, the less likely she is to go crazy the first time she gets a taste of independence as a teen.

Hold hands.

Around the time she turns two years old, thunderstorms will start to scare her. So will house flies, heights, loud noises, dogs, dust bunnies, and pretty much anything unfamiliar. Your job is to comfort her with your presence, and help her learn the difference between rational and irrational fears.

Never stop pursuing her. This is just as important when she's a giggling little girl as it is when she's a difficult teen.

Teach her to roar like a lion. Seriously. Do it. This may come in handy later when she starts to attract the interest of young men.

Teach her to drive. Your approval is just as important as the instructions you give. Remember this if she starts crying while attempting to parallel park.

Whoever said diamonds were a girl's best friend, obviously never met a girl with a dog. Remember this the next time you're near a pet shop.

Buy her a glove and teach her to throw a baseball. Make her proud to throw like a girl . . . a girl with a wicked slider.

Fatherhood is a front-loaded endeavor. Your favorite team, your career, your TV, and your hobbies will always be there. Your daughter, on the other hand, will eventually move out. Prioritize your time.

Give her the freedom to disagree and get angry with you. While not always easy to live with, a little girl who's encouraged to stand up for and express her convictions at home will usually do the same at school, in her career, while dating, and in all her various relationships the rest of her life.

Take it easy on the presents for her birthday and Christmas. Instead, give her the gift of experiences you can share together.

She will lose your car keys one day. Plan accordingly.

Bridie Murray

Girls who are physically active are less likely to engage in promiscuous sexual activity, drop out of school, or put up with abuse. Get her involved in sports at a young age.

At two years old, she has the ability to talk from before sunrise to past sunset. Try to keep up.

Annaleise Mitchell

Take her shoe shopping. Little girls love a new pair of shoes. Then again, so do big girls. You really can't go wrong with this one.

Talk with her often about who she is, where she came from, and the woman she wants to be some day.

Ice cream covers over a multitude of mistakes. Know her favorite flavor and treat her when she makes those mistakes.

Her first crush is coming soon. There's nothing you can do to be ready for it. The sooner you accept this fact, the easier it will be.

When she's little, you're job is to protect her from sharp objects, open flames, skinned knees, and speeding automobiles. As she gets older, what she really needs is someone who'll look out for her emotions.

Stopping to smell the roses from time to time is always a good idea, but sometimes a dandelion is more fun.

Be careful how often you tell her to hurry up. One day you may wish you'd slowed down.

The first time she leaves your house on a date, you may feel a little scared, nervous, and sad. This is perfectly natural.

Always add a few extra marshmallows to her hot chocolate. Small gestures communicate big love.

Beam with pride when she succeeds. Reassure her when she fails. A girl whose dad walks beside her in both will rarely have a problem with either.

Let her know she can always come home. No matter what.

Learn to chase her. Those legs may be little, but they can also be deceptively fast.

When you take her to the beach for the first time, she will probably try to eat the sand. Don't freak out when it happens. Just remember her next diaper will be filled with cement.

FACT: For most little girls, a sheet of stickers is worth more than all the riches in the world. Use this knowledge to your advantage.

Look for ways to encourage her natural curiosity.

Take her with you the next time you buy a major appliance. Make sure she hears you when you tell the salesman, "I'll buy it today if you'll throw in a new playhouse for my daughter."

Build a snowman together. It may be freezing outside, but you'll both be warm where it matters most.

She will climb as high as you let her. Never impose artificial limits.

There is nothing better than an old-fashioned tire swing. **Warning:** Be careful of spinning, especially after lunch.